From the Stones

Brenda Fitzmaurice and Mary Kennelly

Evensong Publications

First Edition
Published by Evensong Publications
2010
Evensong Publications, Radharc Na Rí, Ballyculhane, Glin, County Limerick, Ireland
email: radharcnari@gmail.com

ISBN 978-0-9566687-0-7

Cover Illustration *From the Stones* (2010) by Brenda Fitzmaurice
Graphic design and photography by Janus Design, Glin, Co Limerick
info@janusdesign.ie
Printed by Walsh Colour Print, Castleisland, Co. Kerry

For

Gabriel and my family

With love

Brenda

For

Fr. John Kennelly

For being such a great uncle and for just being there

Mary

Index

Foreword

Brenda and Mary have known each other for more years than either of them would care to remember or to admit – although Brenda thinks Mary may only have been eight years old when they first met! Throughout the years that followed they were aware of, and admirers of, each other's work.

They worked together over a number of years for the **Brendan Kennelly Summer Festival**. In 2005, Brenda held a solo exhibition in the Limerick County Gallery. The exhibition was inspired by the Shannon river estuary and by the landscapes that are washed by it. In response to the paintings, Mary wrote a poem on the same theme and dedicated it to Brenda. Brenda used the poem on her exhibition invitations.

The idea to collaborate grew from this time, but like a fine wine took a little while to mature.

They began working together in 2008. They were inspired by the places and people of their shared surroundings. They chose the title **'From the Stones'** to reflect the extent to which they are products of the nurturing landscape in which they live.

Brenda and Mary are deeply grateful for the help and support which they have received in getting to the point of publication.

They would like to sincerely thank the following:

Their husbands and children, their extended families, their friends;

The people who generously surrendered paintings from their private collections to be photographed and used in this volume and to **Jim Brassil** for his photographs;

Their mentors; for Brenda - **Helena McMahon** and **Cathy Callan**

            for Mary - **Gabriel Fitzmaurice**, **Paddy Kennelly** and **J.B. Keane**.

They wish to thank **Des Kenny** for his introduction and to thank **Ann Egan**, **Jo Slade** and **Declan Kiberd** for their kind words. Their particular thanks go to Tom Moore of **Janus Design** whose input both organisationally and creatively was invaluable.

Introduction

Many years ago a young woman, to whom I sent packages of Irish poetry books every other month, sat in my office and requested that I send her no more poetry written by women. Somewhat taken aback by the request, I asked why? To which she replied: "Because they are not romantic enough."

Her answer has intrigued me ever since but it is only when I read through this collection, 'From the Stones', that I came close to a sense of its deeper meaning. The whole concept of womanhood remains for most men, and some women, something of a mystery and therefore something to be approached with caution. Because of this miscomprehension there is a tendency to either stereotype or idolise the gender leading to prejudice or infatuation. The true spirit and reality of what it is to be a woman is totally ignored.

The subtitle to this collection – A Homage to Place through Painting and Poetry – is somewhat misleading. The poems and the paintings do reflect the North Kerry landscape certainly, but the real "Place" of this book is the female of the human species in all her vicissitudes and to open its pages is to fully experience the sinew, heart and soul of woman with no punches pulled. For the unwary traveller it is a journey fraught with physicality, pain, suffering, tenderness, beauty, loneliness, motherhood, girlhood, wonder, disillusion, maturity, love, hate and self-fulfilment characterised by a driving energy that leaves the reader breathless.

The depth of the female experience present in these pages is such that to fully appreciate the total humanity of the gender, the book needs to be read several times. Personally it is an honour and privilege to invite you to visit this shrine with the caveat that it carries with it a health warning but with the full assurance that it is a journey well worth taking as it greatly enriches our knowledge and understanding of the wonder that is Woman.

"From the Stones" is a book that deserves, nay demands, our deepest respect.

Des Kenny

Whisperings

There was never any doubt
That the stones would talk
To me again in dreams,
When I am planted as I am
With a view of where
Great kings once walked.
In the cold grey stone of castle walls
Their story is kept safe.
There is no rush for them,
The dead learn patience in the grave
Where even rotting takes its time.
They know of time, what I do not,
So they can stand to wait
Until I am made to hear their life,
As the whispers of old ghosts,
On the wind and the singing tide.

Lislaughtin from Saleen   *Oil on Canvas   30cm x 41cm 2006*

Inside I Tremble   *Acrylic on Canvas   41cm x 30cm 2010*

Ten is Half of Twenty

Daughter, soon you will be ten,
Your childhood is now half flown.
Your legs and arms impossibly long
For any child of mine.
A careless almost teenage
Shrug of your head
At odds with eyes filled still
With the world of a younger girl.
From your first, soft, warm breath
I became for you,
And now that you will soon be ten
I realize that my time for letting go
Must begin before I can possibly accept.
I laugh as you blow out your candles
- Inside I tremble.

Penestin 2002

Not for us the mad heat and madder crowds
Of Brittany in July and August.
We come instead to Penestin in September.
With all children, save our own, gone back to school
We come with older folk to play.
The beach we share with scavengers
Of all that is the ocean's gift to give.
And it is here, with sun accentuating
Smells of fresh baked bread and good white wine,
That we as family shake off the thousand
Cares and worries of our days back home.
We learn again to smile more freely and
Give our thanks for simple things
Like children's silly water games
And the warmth of laughing eyes.

Sailboats   *Oil on Canvas   24cm x 30cm   2005*

Matters of the Heart

On Valentine's Day, David Hanley
Read one of Shakespeare's sonnets
On Morning Ireland and we exchanged
Cards and promises for a sweet later on.
The world held its breath, as Hans Blix
Reported on arms in Iraq, and when it was over
Both sides hardened their hearts.
When the news came to me I left straight away.
My loved one well understands that there
Are other, different, older loves that call
From the cradle and can't be denied.
Once there I could see that his heart
Was worn from bereavements, baptisms, betrayals,
Burying children, parents and friends,
In search at all times for his silent God.
On Valentine's Day his heart was attacked.

Hospital Bouquet   *Acrylic on Canvas   30cm x 41cm   2007*

Frisson

We pass, in that narrow corridor,
Close enough to catch each other's scent.
My eyes reflect the hunger in his glance.
That look of his is strong enough to crawl
Inside my skin and fast become a fire,
I burn and blaze and ebb and flow.

It doesn't take five seconds
To reach my husband's side and know
- What a lifetime's wishful thinking won't forget -
That even in our love filled early days
No look of his has ever had the power
To make me burn like that.

Fenit Lighthouse   *Acrylic on Linen   41cm x 61cm   2009*

The Lighthouse

Waiting,
 I am always waiting,
For new stories to pass
Me by on the breeze.
Watching, I am always watching,
For the iron ladies
Floating through my seas.
They whisper softly to me
Secret tales from
A far off shore,
They pity me my stillness,
That I must stay
While they can go.
But I know this is my place,
I could not be
Myself in any other.
This place has made me
What I am – I am
Sky and wind and water.

Hard Day   *Acrylic on Canvas   61cm x 41cm   2010*

Today

Today is hard.
I don't know why.
Today I cannot
Climb out from underneath
A thousand little slights.
Today there is no colour
And no music in my world.
Today is hard
Laughter is a million
Miles away or yet to come.
Today a tear is just
Too hard to find.
Today I am too tired,
Today I am used up.
Today is hard.

Lislaughtin Window to Eternity   *Oil on Canvas   35cm x 45cm   2007*

Insight

While I went with my mother
To do the thousand things that must be done,
Their mother talked softly to them
Of angels and of travelling on,
Then she packed them off to granny's house
To be insulated from all that was to come.
When I saw her, the eldest,
Wide eyed and overwhelmed,
My heart warmed for the first time in three days.
She made her way through noisy crowds
Carrying a cellophane wrapped red rose goodbye
To where we sat in the very front row.
I held her hand, for my sake more than hers
While she struggled to understand,
The crowd, the words, black suits and red eyes.
With her free hand she tugged my sleeve,
She pointed shyly and whispered, afraid to raise her voice,
"Is that my Grandad in that box?"

Humpty Dumpty

After fate had taken down my wall
I fell apart and bled into the ground.
When all the king's horses
And all the king's men
And all their well-intentioned wives,
Found that no amount of hot sweet tea
Could put me back together again,
They suggested that I pull myself together.
Broken people, it would seem,
As well as broken eggs,
Are nothing more than so much mess
To those who are intact.
So I stuck my fifty thousand bits
Into a crazy paving, hollow shell.
That made them smile and say
"We told you all along, that time
Would heal whatever wounds you had."
Well, perhaps.
But let's just wait and see
How long the cellotape will last.

Fish in Deep Water   *Oil on Canvas   20cm x 20cm   2004*

My Grandfather Waits   *Acrylic on Canvas   41cm x 41cm 2010*

My Grandfather Waits . . .

I went and sat with my grandfather
In my father's Hillman Hunter car,
To wait, with him, for the drive to first mass
- As usual he had been over far too early
And only sat outside to put a little extra
 Pressure on my father-
His huge hand swallowed mine,
As much I think to keep me quiet
As show how much he cared.
Its coldness made me look.
His translucent, tissue paper skin
Showing a strange world within
Of blue veined criss-cross roads
Drunkenly leading to and from
Mottled purple cities.
I remember thinking clearly
That these are how dead hands would look.
Of course I did not understand
That after eighty years and now
Without her by his side,
My grandfather had grown tired.
So I just let him hold my hand
And thought it strange
That he already had the hands of a corpse.

The Drive to Lyre *for Alan*

Out from Listowel
And up, up, up
Through narrow, winding,
Drunken roads, hemmed
In by flanks of green,
The boy and his father
And old Johnny, make their
Way to Lyrecrompane.
Past the crazy church,
That planted itself where
The road should have been
And the shop that
Sold ice-cream at

The end of their day.
They go on without stop
Until that gate.
"Hop out there, Nallo,"
Was his father's command.
Every time his heart sank
With the swinging gate.
Beyond any hope of reprieve
He sat back into the car
Alive to the sound
Of Johnny's whistled joy.
Not long to go now-
To their day in the bog.

Smouldering Bog   *Acrylic on Canvas   24cm x 35cm   2010*

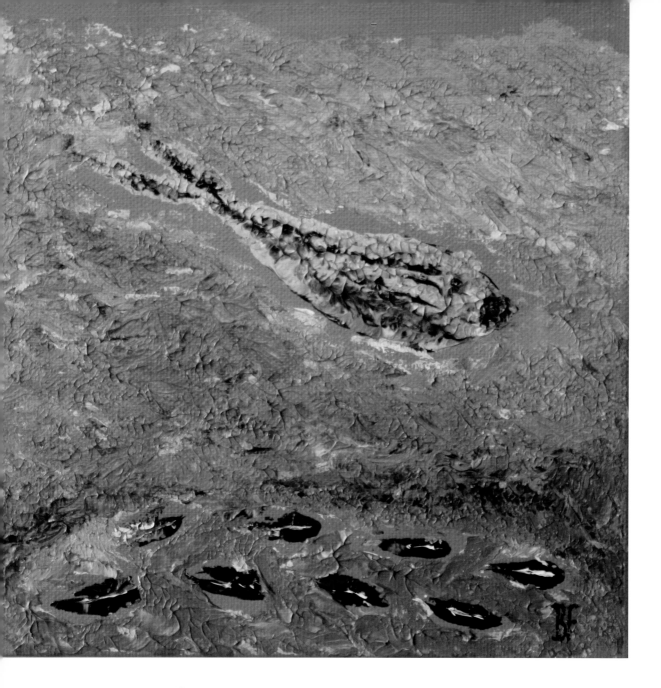

Self Portrait   *Oil on Canvas   20cm x 20cm 2004*

Twins

1

Born early
Through blood and pain.
The midwife took
Her baby girls
And gave them names
She did not choose.
Then they were gone,
Ripping out her heart,
Blighting her womb
To all other life -
Until they took that
From her too.
She dreamed of them
As women,
The night before she died,
At eighty-two.

11

He was always handy
With his hands
- Not a man of words.
What words could have forced
The awful blackness
In his chest to go away?
Instead he made their coffin
On the kitchen table,
Praying through his work.
He planed the wood
Until it was fine enough
For tiny little girls.
He handed them over
To the priest,
To the earth,
To each other.

111

What does any daughter
Understand of sisters
She has never known -
Of what is death and
Of who is in that box?
But she understands
Distance alright
And how they would not
Play or laugh with her -
That she was not enough.
When she is grown
She'll make a family of her own
Her children will know laughter
And know their mother's touch.
She'll leave the coldness
Of the grave behind.

Moon Over Beagh Castle   *Oil on Canvas   40cm x 30cm   2008*

Magdalene

My name,
When He said it,
Became a caress,
Rolling across His tongue,
Playing with His lips,
Warming His eyes
And my blood,
Creating an us
That was painful for those
Who loved Him so much
That they gave up their boats.
So I understood
When they silenced my name
In their story.
But a name, like a story,
Has a life of its own
And Thomas and James

Whispered mine.
Until smaller men
Who had not known Him,
In fear, named me whore,
Giving birth to a lie,
That found life of its own.
Yet something of me
Survived even that.
But the worst,
Was the hurt
Of young girls
For their loving -
And the theft of their babies
All done in my name.
This has soiled me,
Reduced me,
I am covered in shame.

Brenda Fitzmaurice

Father

Father, who will I be
When you are gone,
You, such a huge part
Of the life that shaped
Me piece by piece
Into everything I am?
Now, with part of that puzzle
Forever missing,
Will I be without beginning,
Cast adrift and incomplete?
Whose daughter will I be?
How can I be mother
If I am no longer child?
Will I struggle desperately
To carry all of you within
Yet in the end, like everybody else,
Be content with carrying
All of you I can?
Father who will I be
When you are gone?

Generation   *Oil on Canvas   30cm x 60cm 2009*

Blossom Time   *Acrylic on Linen   24cm x 41cm 2009*

Eye of the Beholder

Here, I am in a woman's world,
A temple of beauty hidden away
From fools who think that nature
Casts her bounty freely over us.
Cleopatra is my sister as I take
My place on beauty's altar.
I am sealed by the warm and perfumed wax
Knowing, as Eve knew, that there is
A price to be paid for wanting more.
Yet I am always unprepared
For the viciousness of the tug
That waters up my eyes and
Clenches both my teeth and nails.
The priestess looks upon her work
And smiles, examining scorched earth-
There are no survivors left.
Aphrodite is echoed in her words
As she continues on her torturous path-
"Beauty feels no pain".

The Battery   *Oil on Canvas   58cm x 48cm   2006*

From the Stones

The day's events are prearranged
This talk in my uncle's pub is one of many
For the visiting group of Americans.
The daytime drinkers at the bar
Smile at first at my antics
"Reading poetry out loud to Yanks!"
Nursing their Guinness
They offer up their own contributions
To the afternoon's entertainment
And our shared audience is left to wonder
How much of this display is choreographed
As one shouts out to my back,
"Vercify us one of your father's then Mary-
By Christ, she didn't bring it from the stones!"

The Battery   *Detail 1 & 2*

When I am finally done one of the visitors
Respectfully asks why I think so many writers
Came from just around these parts.
When I think about it later on I realize
My drunken friend was wrong.
Where else could the music have come from
Living as we do in the shadow of castles?
Where else but from the stones, licked black
By the savage Atlantic and the tidal Shannon estuary,
Teaching us everything we can possibly know
About incessant rhythms?
Where else if not from the stones and the sea and
The skinning wind forever giving and taking
Lifetimes of story?

Winter Meadow   *Oil on Canvas   31cm x 26cm   2005*

Imperfect Fairytale

This is a smaller thing
- Not the fairytale kind of love
Young girls might dream about-
Damaged, filled with distance.
At times we are unsure
If it is worth the trial.
No, this is not the fairytale,
But it remains love just the same.

Visiting my Aunts

I do not know why, more and more,
I hear them call me out to visit them.
But, for the love of them, I go.
I sit silently and listen as they share
Whatever wordless mysteries they will.
And always I remember the first visit
That I made, as a child,
 With my indomitable grandmother,
Who abruptly stopped and said;
"Here are your aunts".
Then the hurricane I knew dissolved,
And the thirty year old mask she wore fell off
As she stood and shook with great big silent sobs,
Until after only a minute she shrugged
And reinserted steel into her spine –
But she never took me there again

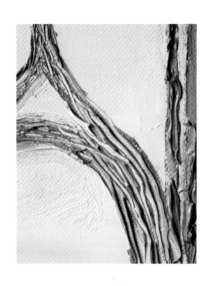

Sacred Space   *Detail 1 & 2*

And she never shared their names,
Even though in the days before she died
She said she often dreamt of them.
It was years before I felt their pull again
And I went there on my own,
As did my mother and my brother,
And we can none of us explain their draw
Or what it is that we receive.
I know only that I am fed and I find peace
While visiting my aunts.
Perhaps that is why I cried when
Fifty five years after they were first
Put in the ground, a headstone finally read;
"for the infant twin daughters
 of Paddy and Bridget Ryan"

Carraigafoyle Castle   *Oil on Canvas   59cm x 48cm   2006*

Carraigafoyle Castle

Time and again I am commanded back
By the whisper of old ghosts
On the grey Atlantic breeze.
Struggling to understand
I press my cheek against cold stone.
I learn that stones tell their own story
While guarding their own secrets,
Tying all who live in their ruined shadow
To other days – generations come and gone.
Glory, power and wealth. Defeat, destruction, death.
The stones the soul survivors.
Witness still to man's great thoughts and deeds
And in the end to man's insignificance.

Songbird

Old friendships needing no false manner,
We sat, we ate, we drank, we laughed.
Until you bade us: "Listen",
- Voice calling from beyond the grave
With the purity of life.
And so we stopped and closed our eyes
And travelled, for just a little time
With you, beyond the rainbow.

(Inspired by Eva Cassidy)

Evening at Saleen   *Oil on Canvas   45cm x 35cm 2006*

Second Sight

At first I did not recognize
That frail old man across the room.
Until distance stripped down the shield
Of memory from across my eyes.
This new recognition is cold
Forcing me to see what I would rather not.
I am afraid.
I am become Eve,
For I too have tasted
Tainted fruit from the forbidden tree
And I am lost to peace.
Your hands are not those hands
Which swung me high into the air
Just to hear my laugh.
Your voice is not the voice that sweetly

Sang of "the pale moon rising"
To send me softly off to sleep
And yet must I live with only now?
I close my eyes
And call upon remembrance
To temper recognition.
I see you once again a golden haired Helios
Striding through my life,
Reminding me that those who
See far must understand
That surface is not all.
I open up my eyes and see-
Yes-our cold today,
Made infinitely more precious
By tomorrow and yesterday.

Going Nature's Way   *Acrylic on Canvas   56cm x 41cm   2008*

A Gentle Healing

There are times, when I gather
Up my wits and charm
And feel myself beloved,
When I am fierce and brave and bright.
In those times I share my joy with you,
And through that sharing find
My countless joys renewed.
But there are times, when I am
Wearied by the fight,
Unable then it seems to find
The smallest chink of light,
And all my countless blessings
Cannot stop me bleeding
From a hundred weeping cuts.
And it is then I need you most
And it is there you make me whole
Until I find that I can laugh again.

Warm Welcome   *Acrylic on Canvas   51cm x 76cm 2009*

Jude

That wounded look
Has been with me
This very long time past,
A more than fitting equal
To all my worst offences,
And it is far more powerful
Than any screaming match.
It says - no dog would
Take the same abuse
That I have given you,
It betrays your disappointment,
That I have thrown away
My hundredth second chance.

It says - you know me now,
That there are no illusions left
To hide my flaws and faults.
But like the patron saint
Of hopelessly lost causes
You give no other outward sign
That you are slowly drowning
 In my constant stream of shit.
You mercifully move
Past it all.
And I will never
Forgive you for it.

When Rooks Fly Homeward   *Oil on Canvas   80cm x 30cm   2006*

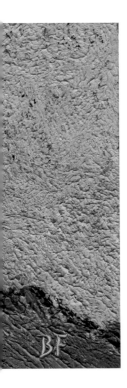

Bedtime Story

Only after you have said one final,
Last, goodbye to everyone,
Do you consent to climb the stairs with me.
After you have finished off your bottle
You are still awake,
And so I lie, your prisoner,
Eyes squeezed shut, jaw clenched,
Making lists of all the jobs that I must do
Before this day's work is done,
Trapped by your happy chatter,
Sit-ups, stories, songs.
I think that you will never rest,
Until, when I no longer expect it soon,
Some almost imperceptible change in breath
Tells me that you have journeyed off,
Perhaps returned to days before the womb,
Or to the glories of your days to come,
Or maybe gone to simple dreams
Of teddy bears and new toy cars –
Wherever – you are gone.
And I, now lonesome, am no longer
Anxious to begin my evening's work.

Blue Shirt   *Acrylic on Canvas   50cm x 70cm 2009*

Preparing for Infidelity

Careful as always she runs the iron
In sweeping strokes over an ice blue shirt,
Bought to reflect the colour of a deceiving eye.
Some internal need demands perfection.
She applies starch to cuffs and collar
Making them almost as stiff as betrayal.
At times she stops and moves the shirt
Along the now warm board, inhaling clean fabric
She knows that shortly it will grace clean skin.
The beauty of both enhanced by a time and effort
And expense long absent from the marriage bed.
She knows too that the next perfumed hand
Upon this shirt will not be hers.
Her final flair is to hang a matching tie
Across her faithless lover's shirt
And add her fervent prayer
That the lying pig might choke on it.

Summer Meadow   *Oil on Canvas   40cm x 30cm 2005*

September

With autumn's still and musky air caressing us,
We escape to our garden, still refusing to recognize its own defeat,
Defiant blooms and golden apples not yet contemplating fall,
Surrounded by the heady smell of slightly wet cut grass,
Onions, carrots, parsnips and potatoes lifted from their beds
And drying out to fill our winter stores.
The cows in the next door field raise their noses
To sniff for sunshine or for rain on the cooling air.
Our children squeal their laughter as they race through
Piles of raked up grass in wellingtons,
Abandoning homework for this evening's outside entertainment.
We gobble up this unexpected meal of joy,
Hoping to lay down supplies to see us through
The unknown separations and disappointments,
Strong words, brittle bones and bitter tears
That life might have in store to test
Our courage, strength and love.
And in those unknown days ahead,
The part of me that does not speak in words
But recognizes greater things it cannot name,
Will offer silent thanks for the ordinary miracles
That we were blessed to share.

Fishy, Fishy   *Oil on Board   40cm x 30cm   1998*

Argument

Round and round and round we go
Like fish in a barrel.
Our argument is an old friend,
It's been with us since we began.
All the lines are tired,
There are no new points of view,
You will not change, I will not leave,
You will be hurt, I will be sad,
But only for a day or two.
Then we will forget,
Or pretend to forget,
And happily go on
Until our friend returns again.

The Bleak Bog Land   *Acrylic on Canvas   61cm x 76cm   2010*

Long Gone

When they hear the news
Malicious minds will rush to tell,
In hushed, shocked whispers,
That you are gone from me.
As usual they peddle a half truth.
Our going from each other
Is evidenced not caused
By your leaving of this house.
And neither of us really knows
When our leaving first began.
Was it you or me that took those
Faltering steps away
And did we understand?
 I think we were together once
But time or use or disappointment
Caused our drip, drip distancing,
The glazing over of my eyes
The closing of your ears.
And we both know another
Cannot come between an us
That is no longer there.
If there was a day when we were one
We have long since been resolutely two.
You are, and have been, gone from me.
I am, and have been, gone from you.

I Wanna Break Free   *Acrylic on Canvas   51cm x 41cm   2010*

Where are you, Rumplestilskin, when you're needed?

The seventeen year old me
In that photograph, has a cocky air
That says, "move over world
Make room for me!
I'm going to travel your lands
And conquer you with the sheer force
Of my personality."
My seventeen year old self is dazzling
Fresh and beautiful – I realize now-
Intoxicated by possibility.
Her cheeky grin mocks the saggy,
Baggy, shaggy thirty-something me.
She could never understand my choices,
The man, the kids, the house,
The cars, the dogs, the cat.
My wild child is buried under
All this bloody respectability,
That, and a mountain of laundry.
 Where are you, Rumplestilskin,
When you're needed
To weave a spell
And set me free?

Sionnan

I was conceived in the cold,
Dark, damp womb of my mother.
Sent forth, to bring life
Those who live upon her face,
I slowly sought daylight
And sang my Siren song
To draw transient humanity
In and on to my unknowable depths.
Sometimes I am mother, sometimes wife
And sometimes murderous, terrifying hag.
Yet I am ever constant
While their countless little lives
Have come and gone.
They break my surface

With their trade
Or spew their poisons
Still I go on,
Long, long after their
Self important rush has stopped
And their bones make
Pretty dust.
I go on,
And on,
And on…
Mysterious, frightening, beautiful,
Constantly renewed and pouring
Into the mouth of my beloved.

Ben at Beale   *Oil on Canvas   30cm x 40cm 2006*

War Wounds

He showed me the scars
From his colourful past
And the false teeth
Which he needed
Because a big ugly prop
Knocked out his front two
On a cold rugby pitch.
So I said "that's alright then
Nobody's perfect"
And I showed him
What gravity had done
To my boobs.
And he ran as fast
As his bandy little
Legs would allow –
In the opposite direction.

Slightly Imperfect   *Oil on Canvas   24cm x 30cm 2005*

A Wet Summer

Two dry, ungrateful flies attempt to
Find a path outside in a drunken
Crazy dance along my patio door,
While beyond, the wooden garden furniture
Takes its own sweet time to rot
In today's latest downpour –
 A sad monument to what we hoped
The summer might have been.
Instead my roses mildewed on the bud and now
The mountain ash is bleeding berries
As the montbretia fires ditches
Full of blackberry coals.
My restless children fight again
Over whose turn it is to watch TV
Or who has spent more time than whom
Playing on their Nintendo Wii.
And tomorrow, hung-over from the rain,
They go back to school.

Another Wet Sunday   *Oil on Canvas   61cm x 48cm   1999*

Hidden Hurt   *Acrylic on Canvas   41cm x 30cm   2010*

Friendship's End

It has been a long time now –
I no longer think my heart will tear
And bleed into the barren soil
Through every weeping pore.
I know it is the truth
To say that life goes on.
I smile, I laugh, I have learnt
That love is possible.
I do not cry for you anymore –
And yet, I am not the same.
Your hurt remains upon my heart
Like some faded red-wine-on-carpet stain,
Almost forgotten, often ignored
Or hidden out of sight,
Scrubbed nearly clean by time,
But always, always, it is there.

Capaill na Mara

I was born listening
To its constant, ever changing song.
At three years old it gripped my ankles
And licked my toes and asked that
It might steal my heart.
No man could ever after that
Claim what was already gone,
Even my children, whom I
Loved as well as any mother could,
Did not own my love in such a way.
It gave me peace, to heal my wounds,
Bounty, beyond my needs or wants,
And viciousness, so that I might know
Great joy in simply being alive,
Sending wild horses to topple me,
Spitting salt to strip my lips and skin,
Screaming at me.
Beside such breathtaking fury
Why should I fear queens or men?

Until I Saw the Sea   *Oil on Canvas   60cm x 60cm   2008*

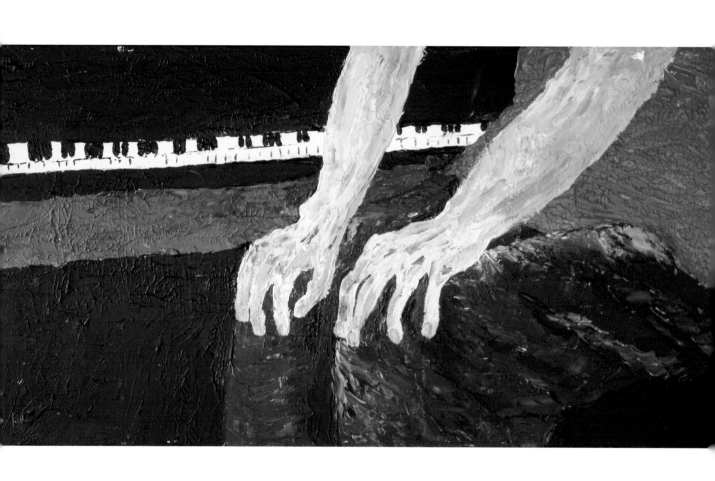

Stolen Music   *Acrylic on Canvas   60cm x 30cm   2010*

Old Age and Penury

What good are all their accolades
When in the end the music slipped away from you?
Gentle as the day slips into night
It went drip, dripping out of you,
Almost as though it had not been
The only constant lover in your life
Since well before you set aside
Those ways that made you child.
Gone now, beyond the recall of all
Your frantic craft and discipline.
It leaves you naked and alone
A feeble squawking shell
Tormented all the time by memory
For once you mastered beauty.

John's Poppy Meadow　　*Oil on Canvas　40cm x 30cm　1999*

Morning Adventurers

He slips away, unknown to his father and to me
- Still clinging desperately to last night's sleep-
His uniform a tee- shirt, nappy and wellington boots
- His older brother's and two sizes too big -
Is hardly enough to protect from a morning
Not yet warmed by the newborn sun.
His troops, two dogs and a cat,
Without being called soon follow behind
As he finds his first stick and cuts swathes
Through the day and the hoards in his mind.
Later, he holds his council of war
In his mother's front flower bed- collateral damage!
Around him the dogs settle down,
Magi with cocked puzzled glances come to adore,
They wag their tails through ornamental poppies.
Where he leads they follow, together there is
A whole wide world for them to explore.

Ophelia

What did the playwright care
For the young girl
Without a mother
Who played too much alone?
Or for the young woman
That my father would see married off,
Listening as my brother and his friends
Laughed out stories
Of the skirts the prince had raised?
And yet my heart would pound
At the briefest glimpse of him.
What did the playwright understand
Of all I risked in trusting him,
Of my delight in loving him,

Of my momentary peace in holding him
Afterwards, as he slept deeply in my arms?
The playwright did not know
The terror I lived everyday,
That he might cast my love aside
And find a better lady in my place.
That fear was why I hid from him
When his mother laughed too long and loud
At jokes her husband's brother
Had no right to tell.
The playwright knew me only
After I had gambled all I was and lost.
He knew me spent, betrayed and floundering.

Winter Dancing

The little boy dances out his joys,
They bubble from inside of him
And two year old limbs,
Not old enough yet to be
Pinned down by earth's
Incessant gravity,
Take flight.
Ten-minute-old woes
Are cast away, forgotten
As he moves now into
The flirting light
Of the winter sun.
Trials that might lie in store
Not half an hour away,
Have no power to touch
This incandescent child,
As he takes his bottle
From his mother's hand
And turns to watch TV.
The little boy dances out his joys.

January Garden   *Acrylic on Canvas   40cm x 30cm   2010*

Anniversary Waltz

- The radio left on,
Cats and dogs fed,
Car ready for the NCT.
For God's sake flush the loo!
Bedtime stories,
Insurance paid,
Hold my hand,
Empty carton in the 'fridge,
Another match to watch,
Compost on the flowers,
You drive me nuts,
My joy, my rock,
Friendship, laughter, tears-
After all these years
I can no longer tell
Which steps are mine
And which are yours.
Is this love?
Are we happy?
Is there something else
That I would ask of you?
What more could you possibly do?

Tarbert Lighthouse   *Oil on Canvas   50cm x 20cm   2005*

The Jealous Sea *for B.F.*

She thought to paint the stones
 And the castles and the chimneys
That stand sentry by the sea,
So I called to her and drew her down;
I entered her, she accepted me.
I taught her all the mysteries
Of my dark and hidden bed,
I flowed through her
And led her on a path,
I knew, she feared to tread.
Then she and I knew loss and gain,
We died and were reborn.
I surrendered up her liquid soul,
Forever altered, and through water
Able to understand solid form.

Brenda Fitzmaurice

Born and raised in Tarbert, Co. Kerry, Brenda was educated at Tarbert National School and at Mount Trenchard, Foynes, Co. Limerick. Following her graduation from Mary Immaculate College in Limerick, she taught for over twenty years in Tarbert National School before pursuing her lifelong passion for painting. She studied art at the Institute of Art Design and Technology and her works are highly praised. Pieces of her artwork hang in many private collections. Primarily a land and seascape artist, her paintings have received critical acclaim for their skilful evocation of the character of her subjects. She exhibits both as a solo artist and in group exhibitions. She has collaborated with poets and writers on book covers and illustrations for texts. She accepts private commissions.

Her solo exhibitions include:

2005 Limerick County Gallery

2006 Brendan Kennelly Summer Festival

2007 Squan Custom Frame Shop, Manasquan, New Jersey

Brenda lives in Moyvane with her husband Gabriel. They have two children John and Nessa.

Brenda may be contacted at;

Applegarth,

Moyvane,

Listowel,

Co. Kerry

email: brenda@brendafitzmaurice.com

www.brendafitzmaurice.com

BF

Mary Kennelly

Mary was born in 1970 and was raised along with her five siblings in the North Kerry village of Ballylongford.

Mary studied theology and history at St. Patrick's College, Maynooth. She studied for the Higher Diploma in Education in University College Galway. In recent times she undertook a Postgraduate Diploma in Learning Support and Special Educational Needs in Mary Immaculate College, Limerick. She has just completed her Masters degree in Educational Management in Waterford Institute of Technology.

She teaches in Presentation Secondary School, Listowel, Co. Kerry. She also works for the Special Education Support Service. She worked in the Arts for many years including time with Writers' Week Listowel and the Brendan Kennelly Summer Festival. She has written features for a number of publications including 'The Kerryman', 'The Sunday Independent' and 'The Sunday Tribune'. She has edited a number of publications. In 2004 she published 'Sunny Spells, Scattered Showers' a collection of poetry and paintings with the artist Rebecca Carroll.

Mary currently lives in Glin, Co. Limerick with her husband Gus and their three children Ruth, Matthew and Caleb.

Mary may be contacted at:

Radharc na Rí

Ballycullane Upper,

Glin,

Co. Limerick.

email: mary@marykennelly.com

www.marykennelly.com